Independence Day

Lori Dittmer

seedlings

CREATIVE EDUCATION • CREATIVE PAPERBACKS

Published by Creative Education and Creative Paperbacks
P.O. Box 227, Mankato, Minnesota 56002
Creative Education and Creative Paperbacks are imprints of
The Creative Company
www.thecreativecompany.us

Design by Ellen Huber; production by Colin O'Dea
Art direction by Rita Marshall
Printed in China

Photographs by Creative Commons Wikimedia (Emanuel
Leutze/Metropolitan Museum of Art, John Trumball/
United States Capitol), Getty Images (Jonathan Rehg/
The Image Bank), iStockphoto (C5Media, Creativeye99,
ferrantraite, ffranny, gilaxia, GlobalP, IrenaStar, KatSnowden,
Valerie Loiseleux, mvp64, Nikada, Pekic, SKLA, TasiPas),
Shutterstock (flysnowfly, Oleksandra Naumenko, Tatiana
Popova)

Library of Congress Cataloging-in-Publication Data
Names: Dittmer, Lori, author.
Title: Independence day / Lori Dittmer.
Series: Seedlings.
Includes index.
Summary: A kindergarten-level introduction to Independence
Day, covering the holiday's history, popular traditions, and
such defining symbols as flags and parades.
Identifiers: LCCN: 2019053297 / ISBN 978-1-64026-331-4
(hardcover) / ISBN 978-1-62832-863-9 (pbk) / ISBN 978-1-
64000-461-0 (eBook)
Subjects: LCSH: Fourth of July—Juvenile literature.
Classification: LCC E286.A12725 2020 / DDC 394.2634—dc23

CCSS: RI.K.1, 2, 3, 4, 5, 6, 7; RI.1.1,
2, 3, 4, 5, 6, 7; RF.K.1, 3; RF.1.1

First Edition HC 9 8 7 6 5 4 3 2 1
First Edition PBK 9 8 7 6 5 4 3 2 1

TABLE OF CONTENTS

Hello, Independence Day! **4**

When Is Independence Day? **6**

Holiday Symbols **8**

Fighting for Freedom **10**

Signing the Declaration **12**

Holiday Food **14**

How Do People Celebrate? **17**

Goodbye, Independence Day! **19**

Picture Independence Day **20**

Words to Know **22**

Read More **23**

Websites **23**

Index **24**

Hello, Independence Day!

This American holiday is about freedom.

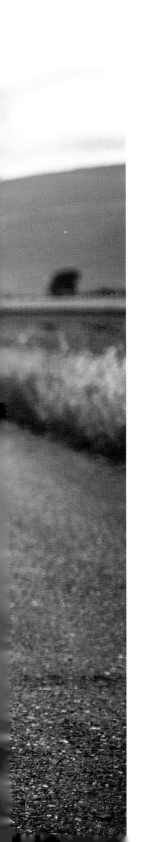

People in the United States celebrate on July 4th.

American flags are red, white, and blue. Flags are everywhere on July 4th.

In 1776, the U.S. was made up of colonies. They were at war with England.

They wanted to be free.

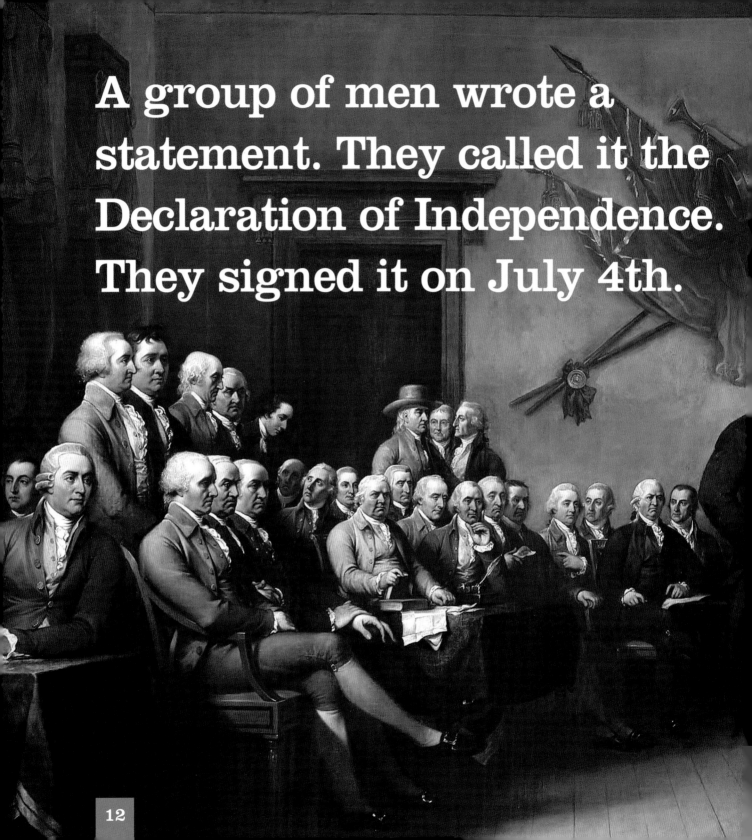

A group of men wrote a statement. They called it the Declaration of Independence. They signed it on July 4th.

Today, people eat outside on the 4th.

They watch parades.

Bands play music. Fireworks light up the sky. People wave flags.

Goodbye, Independence Day!

Picture Independence Day

American flag

Liberty Bell

fireworks

bald eagle

colonies: areas controlled by another country

freedom: the right to act, speak, or think as one wants without being controlled

Read More

Grack, Rachel. *Independence Day.*
Minneapolis: Bellwether Media, 2018.

Manley, Erika S. *Independence Day.*
Minneapolis: Jump!, 2018.

Websites

DKfindout: Independence Day
https://www.dkfindout.com/us/more-find-out/festivals-and
-holidays/independence-day/
Read more about Independence Day and the Declaration.

National Geographic Kids: Independence Day
https://kids.nationalgeographic.com/explore/history
/independence-day/
Learn about the history of the American colonies.

Index

Declaration of
   Independence 12
England 10
freedom 6, 11
history 10–11, 12
symbols 8, 17
timing 7, 8, 12
traditions 14, 15, 17